北京胡同

The Hutongs of Beijing

北京の胡同

中国旅游出版社
China Travel & Tourism Press

序

它是唯一的
北京胡同是中国唯一的
北京胡同是世界唯一的
独一无二　仅此一家
所以不能毁
只能保
要特别珍惜
不要让大家都有的代替了唯一的

它是美丽的
北京胡同是有总体设计构思的
不是胡来的
北京胡同规规矩矩
永远正东正西正南正北
北京胡同有树当它的陪衬
宛如镶着花边
北京胡同以灰色为基调
古雅而朴实
清淡而庄重

它是先进的
北京胡同闹中取静　处处有空
是典型意义上的居住区
北京胡同有田园品格　贴近自然
是天人合一的杰作
北京胡同是城市中心的别墅群体
是现代都市理想的模式
北京胡同满载阳光、空气和水
是兼顾隐私和保护人际谐合要求的妙方

它是历史的
北京胡同已经八百岁
北京胡同里有数不尽的好建筑
处处都有人文故事
撒满了文物古迹
北京胡同是中华优秀文化传统的光辉载体和橱窗
北京胡同是历史遗留给今人的金疙瘩

中国现代文学馆馆长　舒乙

仅以此短句片语权当《北京胡同》画册的小序
2002.4　于中国现代文学馆

Foreword

By Shu Yi

Beijing's hutongs are famous not only in China but also in the whole world. We must therefore preserve these architectural treasures instead of allowing modern skyscrapers to replace them.

The hutongs have a charm of their own. They follow careful construction plans and rules of architecture. Gray is the main tone of the tree-lined hutongs, which adds to their simultaneous elegance and simplicity.

Beijing's hutongs are typical residential districts, which provide relief from the noise and pollution typical of urban surroundings, and offer more space and freedom. They are more in tune with nature, thus illustrating the concept of man as a part of nature and proposing an ideal alternative to a large, bustling metropolis. This safeguards people's privacy and at the same time, promotes tranquility.

These residential districts have a history of 800 years. Brilliant showcases of China's glorious culture and traditions, Beijing's hutongs are among the most valuable symbols of our rich heritage.

April 2002, Chinese Contemporary Literature Museum

* Shu Yi is director of Chinese Contemporary Literature Museum

はしがき

それは唯一のものである
北京の胡同は中国唯一のものであり
世界唯一のものである
独一無二のもので、北京を除いてどこにもない
だから壊してはならず
保存することしかできない
特別に大切にしなければならず
みながもっているもので唯一のものに取って代わらせてはならない

それは美しいものである
北京の胡同は総体的に設計、構想されたものであり
いい加減につくったものではない
北京の胡同はきちょうめんなもので
すべて真東と真西、真南と真北に走っている
北京の胡同にあしらいとして木が植えてあり
あたかも胡同にはめた模様のついたわくのようである
北京の胡同の色はほとんど灰色であり
灰色は古めかしく、上品、素朴であり
あっさりして荘重である

それは先進的なものである
北京の胡同は賑やかさの中に静けさがあり、いたるところが空いており
典型的な居住区である
北京の胡同は田園の品格があり、自然に近づいており
天然と人工が一つに合わさった傑作である
北京の胡同は都市の中にある別荘群であり
近代的都市の理想的なモデルである
北京の胡同に陽光、空気、水がいっぱいあり
プライバシーを配慮し、対人関係の和合を保護するよい方法である

それは歴史的なものである
北京の胡同は八百年の歴史があり
すばらしい建築が数え切れないほどあり
いたるところに人文の故事があり
文物や古跡があまねく分布している
北京の胡同は中華の優れた文化的伝統の輝かしいキャリアーとショーウィンドーであり
歴史が今の人に残した宝である

謹んでこの短い文で画集『北京の胡同』のささやかなはしがきとする

２００２年４月 中国現代文学館にて
中国現代文学館館長 舒 乙

不管您是初到北京的客人，还是久别故都的游子，相信您一定会抽暇到饱含京味儿的小胡同，或结伴漫游，或骑自行车、坐三轮车旅游，欣赏古老的京都神韵，追怀幽远的胡同情思……

我们向您奉献的这本《北京胡同》画册，就是从不同侧面为您展现古都北京胡同的独特魅力，讲述胡同里千奇百怪的故事。

“胡同”，是贯通城市干道的网络，中国的其它城市一般都称其为“坊”、“里”、“弄”、“巷子”等，只有北京才把小巷称为胡同。

说起北京胡同的起源，要追溯至元代大都城的建置。

公元1215年，成吉思汗的蒙古军队，一把大火将金代皇宫焚烧成一片废墟。后来，成吉思汗的孙子——元世祖忽必烈，来到曾为金中都的燕京，在其东北郊外的一片水域之畔，重新修筑了大内灵囿及隆福、兴圣三宫，环绕三座宫殿修筑了一道城墙，就是后来的皇城。围绕这个核心又确定了以钟鼓楼为北边起点，直达大都城南门的城市中轴线。在全城设九条南北走向和东西走向的干道。并在此基础上，随着城市居民生活的不断变迁，形成后来规划方整的棋盘式的胡同。

北京的胡同和四合院是历代北京人的安身立命之所，北京人离不开胡同、四合院，而胡同、四合院也在历代北京人不断变化的生存条件下，在不断演进、发展、变化……

至于胡同中的各色人物，七十二行、规门里道、家长里短，是祖祖辈辈北京人从生活中创造出来的京味儿文化的体现。当您在北京胡同里畅游，当您以独特的视角审视胡同的现在与过去，当您的精神和情感在新与旧中沟通，在沉淀的往事中升华之时，您一定会心旷神怡，浮想联翩，游兴倍增。

Dear reader, whoever you may be - a tourist visiting Beijing for the first time or a Beijinger who has just come back after a long, long absence - you will surely find time to explore Beijing's hutongs (side lanes) in a group or alone, by bicycle or pedicab, to enjoy the unique hutong culture of this ancient city.

This album The Hutongs of Beijing will tell you the fascinating stories of Beijing's hutongs from different angles and about their changes over the past centuries.

Hutongs are known as streets, lanes, and alleys in other cities in China, and they form the skeleton of old Beijing. Their history can be traced back to the Yuan Dynasty (1279-1368) when the Mongols built Dadu (the Great Capital), which later became Beijing.

In 1215, Mongol troops led by Genghis Khan attacked the Jin Tartars and burned down their palace in Zhongdu or Yanjing (the Central Capital of Jin) in what is now Beijing. Khublai Khan, the grandson of Genghis Khan, built a group of three palatial structures by the waterside on the northwestern outskirts of Zhongdu as the center of his new capital and encircled the area with a city wall. The central axis of the capital city ran from Zhonggulou (Bell and Drum Towers) in the north to the city gate in the south. There were nine north-south and nine east-west streets intersecting each other and dividing the city into rectangular blocks of single-story houses grouped around courtyards.

Hutongs and their courtyard houses (known as siheyuan in China) have been the home of Beijing residents through the ages, but as time goes by, they are changing.

Many hutongs were named after the markets or trades once conducted along them. Others took their names from famous people. Beijing's hutong culture is part of the culture created by Beijing residents generation after generation. If you make a tour of the hutongs, you will better understand their past and present and have a great deal of fun as well.

初めて北京に来たお客さんであろうと、または長い間都を離れていた人であろうと、きっと暇を見つけては、北京の風韻にあふれる小さな胡同(路地)を連れと一緒に気のむくままに歩き回ったり、あるいは自転車か輪タクに乗って遊覧して、古都の雰囲気にひたり、はるか昔の胡同への思いを追懐したりするものと信じる。

『胡同の景観』と題するこの画集は、とりもなおさず異なる側面から古都北京の胡同のもつ独特な魅力を展示し、胡同をめぐるいろいろの不思議な物語について述べている。

「胡同」は都市の幹線道路を貫通するネットワークであり、中国のその他の都市では一般には「坊」、「里」、「弄」、「巷子」などと称されているが、北京だけが小さな路地を胡同と呼んでいる。

北京の胡同の起源は、元代の大都城の建造にまでさかのぼる。

1215年、ジンギス汗の率いるモンゴルの軍隊は、火を放って金朝の王宮を灰燼に帰させた。その後、ジンギス汗の孫、元の世祖フビライは、かつて金朝の中都であった燕京に来て、その北東郊外の水域のほとりに内裏の霊囿および隆福、興聖の三つの宮殿を再建し、この三つの宮殿を囲むようにして城壁を築いた。これはその後皇城と呼ばれるようになった。これを中心として、鐘鼓楼を北側の起点とし、南の城門に至る都市の中軸線を確定した。全城に南北と東西に走る九本の幹線道路を建設した。これを基礎として、都市住民の暮らしがたえず変化するにつれて、碁盤のように四角く整然とした胡同が形成された。

北京の胡同と四合院(四角形の庭を囲んで、東西南北の四面にある四棟の建物で構成される住宅)は、歴代の北京人が身を寄せるところであり、北京人は胡同と四合院を離れることができず、胡同と四合院も、歴代の北京人のたえず変化する生存条件の下で、たえず進化、発展、変化した。

胡同にあるさまざまな人物、あらゆる生業、住宅や通路などは北京人が先祖代代生活の中でつくり出した北京の風韻をもつ文化を具現している。北京の胡同をのんびりと歩き、独特な視角で胡同の現在と過去を注意深く見る時、あなたの精神と感情が新しいものと古いものを介して通い合い、沈殿した往事の中で昇華する時、きっと気分が広々として爽やかになり、いろいろのことを思い浮かべ、遊覧の興味が倍増するであろう。

枝繁叶茂的树木，烟雨空濛的景观，洗去了昔日京城胡同“无风三尺土，有雨一街泥”的旧容。

A hutong after a rain. In former days, the hutongs in Beijing were unpaved. They were "dusty on fine days and muddy on rainy ones," as an old saying goes.

枝葉が生い茂る木々に霧雨がそぼ降る景観は、「風が吹かない時は土が三尺も積もり、雨が降ると通りが泥まみれになる」という昔の北京の姿を洗い流した。

①

①春节，是中国最重要的传统节日。看，门上的挂钱儿（门笺）、门神、春联，红红火火，使古老的民居再次焕发了青春。

A doorway during Spring Festival, the most important festival in China. It is the custom of Beijingers to paste Spring Festival couplets, pictures of the door god, and auspicious characters on the gateposts and door panels on that occasion.

春節は中国の最も重要な伝統的祝日である。ごらんなさい。門の上にある挂銭児（門箋）、門神、春聯は、とても賑やかで、古い民家は再び青春を取り戻した。

②孩子上学了，大人上班了，那倚墙而立的自行车和横斜路中的平板车，为小胡同增添了几分宁静。摄于东城区茶儿胡同。

Char (Tea) Hutong. Beijing's hutongs are quiet on weekdays as the schoolchildren and most of the adults are away from their homes. The bicycles and pedicabs parked against the wall and in the middle of the hutong add to the quiet atmosphere.

子供たちが学校へ行き、大人たちが出勤したあと、壁際においてある自転車と胡同に斜めにおいてある荷物運搬用の三輪車は、小さな胡同にいくぶんかの静けさを添えている。東城区の茶児胡同で撮影。

②

畅游北京胡同

Hutong Culture

北京城是完全按照中国传统哲理进行规划、设计和营建的，在一些细微之处可以体现出皇权的威严及市民文化的形态。

从空中鸟瞰，可以看见以紫禁城为中心，有一条从永定门到钟、鼓楼全长7.8公里的南北中轴线，与此中轴线相配，有南北方向的大街，东西方向则有众多的胡同，形成棋盘式的街道网络，并由城楼、坛台、庙宇、旧王府等构成丰富多彩的街道景观。

串北京的小胡同，犹如进入了大观园。那古老的寺庙白塔，伴着幽幽长巷；那胡同里的门楼、影壁、门墩儿，装点着寻常百姓家；那跨海越湖的银锭桥，诉说着纷繁往事；那夹道的参天古树，佐证着悠久的胡同历史……

串北京的小胡同，有时又仿佛进入了多姿多彩的画廊。在那晨昏晴雨、春夏秋冬景色的变化中，展示着古都的独特风韵。

串北京的小胡同，更像进入了博物馆，那丰厚的文化底蕴令人叹为观止。胡同两旁的宅院大门，形形色色：八字粉墙，门大漆亮，那是昔日官宦和富户的住宅；大门设在外檐柱间，门框两侧砌砖墙，门楣两侧饰如意图案的砖雕，暗喻着“吉祥如意”。它有大小、高低之分，住户千差万别。胡同中最小型的门楼是直接开在院墙开口处的墙垣式大门，也叫随墙门，这种门楼与墙相连，门楣、屋面、脊饰都比较简单朴素，是小型四合院和三合院的大门，住户多为平头百姓。此外，胡同两旁，大门里外的门礅儿、影壁、砖雕、石刻，更是丰富多彩，它们在幽静的胡同中沐浴了千百年风雨，阅尽了人间沧桑。

北京内城西北部地区的众多地名，如，朝天宫，马市桥、四牌楼、毛家湾、蒋养房以及火药局胡同、王奶奶胡同等，异采纷呈。其实，这一带还有许多更新鲜、奇怪的胡同名称，如：三不老胡同，针尖胡同，十八半截胡同，大月牙胡同等。在其它城区也有些胡同名称，更是趣味横生，如：闷葫芦罐胡同、耳朵眼儿胡同，九道湾胡同、小椅子圈胡同、车道沟胡同……这些胡同，一般都是根据当时的地形、地貌及实际情况而命名的。这些随口而出的胡同名字，既是通俗、幽默的京味语言，又是最原始、最具有京味儿特色的胡同名称。

此外，因名人居住、历史事件等命名的胡同也占有一定比例。如：三不老胡同是因为明代七下西洋的三保太监郑和曾居住在这里而得名，只不过是由“三保老爷”而讹传成“三不老”；灵境胡同是清代林清起义，震撼了皇朝，人们将“林清”谐音为“灵境”，以纪念这段史实。还有些胡同因原名不雅而谐音改叫的，如“小哑吧”改为“小雅宝”，王寡妇改为“王广福”，鸡罩改为“吉兆”。

知道了这些胡同名称的来历，再对照一幅幅胡同实景的图片，您可以大致领略到北京胡同所包涵的地域特征和丰厚的文化底蕴。

The old city of Beijing was built according to a plan based on Chinese philosophy. It symbolized imperial authority on the one hand and showed folk culture on the other.

Viewing the city from the air, one can find a north-south central axis, 7.8 kilometers long, running through the entire city from the Bell and Drum Towers in the north to Yongdingmen (Gate of Eternal Pacification) in the south.

Beijing's principal avenues and streets mostly run north and south. They are intersected by hutongs running east and west to divide the city into a grid. The hutongs along with the towers of the city gates, the altars, the temples, and the former mansions of princes constitute the unique cityscape of Beijing.

Many of Beijing's quiet hutongs have interesting stories behind them. It seems that even the white dagobas, the pavilions on Jingshan Hill, the tall, old pines and cypresses, the decorated archways, and the graceful white marble bridges across the rivers and lakes recount the past of the city and its hutongs.

Beijing's hutongs look like kaleidoscopic galleries. They seem to change with the seasons and even with the time of day.

The size of the front gate of a courtyard house originally depended on the owner's status. Large, brightly painted gates with high walls surrounding the compound were for high-ranking officials and the rich. Most front gates lead into short passages with walls on both sides. They are called ruyimen (good luck gate) because the walls above them and the roof ridges are decorated with bricks carved with auspicious patterns. The front gate of a siheyuan or a sanheyuan inhabited by ordinary people was much smaller, and the decorations on its roof ridges were simple or nonexistent.

When touring the hutongs in Beijing, one can still find a large number of screen walls, brick carvings, and stone sculptures flanking the gate of a siheyuan. They are, in fact, eyewitnesses to the vicissitudes of the hutongs and courtyard houses in the old city.

The names of places in Beijing are especially interesting. In the northwestern part of the inner city of old Beijing, for

北京の胡同を ゆっくり遊ぶ

example, are Chaotiangong (Heaven-Worshiping Temple), Mashiqiao (Horse-Market Bridge), Sipailou (Four Archways), Maojiawan (Mao Family Bend), Huoyaoju Hutong (Gunpowder-Office Alley), and Wangnainai Hutong (Granny Wang Alley). Some hutongs have strange names like Sanbulao (He-Who-Never-Grows-Old-in-Three-Aspects Alley), Zhenjian (Pinpoint Alley), and Dayueyar (Greater Crescent Moon Alley).

Hutongs with interesting names can also be found in other parts of the city. Some examples are Menhuluguanr Hutong (Piggybank Alley), Erduoyanr Hutong (External Opening of the Ear Alley), Jiudaowan Hutong (Nine-Bend Alley), Che dao gou Hutong (Rutted Path Alley). Most of the hutongs were named after their shapes and locations. Their names are easy to pronounce, popular with the common people, and rich in Beijing folk culture.

In addition, many of the names of hutongs are associated with famous people or historical events. Sanbulao Hutong was named after Zheng He, who, also known as Zheng Sanbao, led a large fleet to call on the various ports of the South China Sea and the ports on the eastern African coast on seven expeditions during the early Ming Dynasty (1368-1644). Originally, it was called Sanbao Laoye, meaning Lord Sanbao Alley. As it was often mispronounced, it gradually became Sanbulao (He-Who-Never-Grows-Old-in-Three-Aspects). Lingjing Hutong (Divine Land Alley) was in fact named after Lin Qing (1770-1813), who started a revolt to topple the Qing Dynasty but failed. It was so named because it sounds roughly the same as the name of the revolt leader.

The names of many hutongs in Beijing have remained unchanged. Some retain the same sound but are written with different homophonic characters, and others have been changed because of unpleasant meanings. For example, Xiaoyaba (Lesser Mute) has been changed to Xiaoyabao (Lesser Elegant Treasure); Wangguafu (Widow Wang) to Wangguangfu (Wang the Blessed); and Jizhao (Chicken Coop) to Jizhao (Good Omen).

北京城は完全に中国の伝統的哲理に従って企画、設計、建造されたもので、細かいところでも王権の威厳および市民文化の状況を具現している。

空から鳥瞰すると、紫禁城を中心に、永定門から鐘鼓楼に至る全長7.8キロの南北中軸線が見える。南北中軸線に合わせて、南北に延びる大通りがあり、東西の方向には、あまたの胡同が碁盤のような街道ネットワークをつくり、また城楼、壇台、廟宇、古い王府などは豊富多彩な街道の景観を織り成している。

北京の小さな胡同を歩き回ると、大観園(『紅楼夢』に書いてある華麗な庭園)に入ったような感じがする。例の古びた仏寺の白塔の下に静かな長い路地があり、胡同の中にある門楼、目隠しの塀、門の土台石は一般庶民の家を飾り立て、いくつもの池にまたがっている銀錠橋は、昔のいろいろのことについて話しているようで、道の両側に高くそびえる古木は、胡同の古い歴史を証明している。

北京の小さな胡同を歩き回ると、多彩な画廊に入ったような感じがする時もある。朝と夕方、晴れた時と雨の降る時、春夏秋冬の景色が変わる中で、古都の独特な風韻を展示している。

北京の小さな胡同を歩き回ると、博物館に入ったような感じがし、その豊富な文化の蘊蓄は人々を賛嘆させるばかりである。胡同両側の住宅の表門はさまざまな形をしている。壁が白く塗られ、八の字の形をしており、門が大きく、漆が塗ってあるのは、役人と金持ちの邸宅であり、表門が軒を支える柱の間にあり、門わくの両側は煉瓦の壁で、門の上にある横木の両側に「吉祥如意」を喩える如意の図案を彫った煉瓦が飾ってある。この門は大きさと高さがまちまちで、住人も千差万別である。胡同の最も小さな門楼は、庭を囲む塀の口の開いているところにつくられた塀式の表門で、隨墻門とも呼ばれている。この種の門楼は塀と連なり、門の上にある横木、屋根、屋根の棟の飾りはいずれもわりに簡単、素朴なもので、小型の四合院と三合院(四合院のうち倒座という南側の建物がないもの)の表門であり、住人はたいてい一般庶民である。このほか、胡同両側の表門の内外にある土台石、目隠しの塀、煉瓦彫刻、石刻などは、なおさら豊富多彩で、静かな胡同の中で長い間風雨にさらされ、世の移り変わりを残らず経てきている。

北京内城北西部の地名は、朝天宮、馬市橋、四牌楼、毛家湾、蒋養房および火薬局胡同、王奶奶胡同などと多彩である。その実、この一帯にはそれよりも珍しく、不思議な胡同の名称もたくさんある。例えば、三不老胡同、針尖胡同、十八半截胡同、大月芽胡同などがそれである。その他の地区の胡同の名称にもっと面白いものがある。悶葫蘆罐胡同、耳朵眼児胡同、九道湾胡同、小椅子圏胡同、車道溝胡同はそのいくつかの例である。これらの胡同は一般には当時の地形、地貌および実際の状況に基づいて命名されたものである。これら口から出まかせの胡同の名称は、通俗的でユーモラスな北京風の言葉でもあれば、最も原始的で最も北京の特色をもつ胡同の名称でもある。

このほか、胡同に住んだ有名人や歴史的出来事などにちなんで命名された胡同も一部分ある。例えば、三不老胡同は明代に七回も南洋に行った三保太監の鄭和がかつて住んだことがあるためにつけられた名称で、「三保老爺」がなまって「三不老」となったにすぎない。霊境胡同は、清代の林清蜂起が王朝を震撼したので、人々はこの史実を記念するため、「林清」の発音をもじって「霊境」という名称をつけたのである。また一部の胡同はもとの名称が奥ゆかしくないために、その発音をもじって別の名称をつけたものもある。例えば、「小唖巴」を「小雅宝」に改め、「王寡婦」を「王広福」に改め、「鶏罩」を「吉兆」に改めるなどがそのいくつかの例である。

これら胡同の名称の来歴を知ってから、さらに胡同の実景を映した写真と対照してみれば、北京の胡同に含まれている地域的特徴と豊富な文化の蘊蓄をおよそ会得することができるだろう。

胡同是由两旁的一座座院落围成的。按照元代的城市规划,大街宽24步（约37米），小巷宽6步（约9米）。岁月悠悠，胡同两旁的建筑，随着主人的变迁，也在不断改变。这家院落的山墙，明显地挤占胡同，类似的情况使北京的胡同变得宽窄不一。

Hutong is a narrow lane with courtyard houses on both sides. According to the city planning of the Yuan Dynasty, the width of an avenue or street should be 24 paces (about 37 meters) and that of a hutong should be six paces (about nine meters). With the passage of time, many hutongs became narrower and narrower because people often encroached on them by expanding their compounds. This courtyard house has extended its walls to the middle of the hutong.

胡同は両側に並んでいる庭に囲まれてできたものである。元代の都市計画によると、大通りの幅は２４歩（約３７メートル）、小さな路地の幅は6歩（約9メートル）である。歳月がたつと、胡同両側の建築も主人の移り変わりにつれてたえず変わっている。この庭の建物の山墻は明らかに胡同にはみ出している。これに似た状況によって、北京の胡同の幅が同じでなく、広いところもあれば、狭いところもある。

徜徉在雪后的胡同中，空气特别清新。

A hutong in the snow.

雪後の胡同をのんびりと歩くと、空気が特別清新のように感ずる。

雪后

A hutong after a snow.

胡同の雪景色。

高墙下的窄巷，反衬出胡同的幽深。

A narrow hutong hemmed in by high walls.

高い壁の下の狭い路地は、胡同の静かさと奥深さを引き立てている。

一场大雪飘白了京城，装点了胡同，树上、房上、墙上洁白一片。

A hutong in the snow.

大雪が降って北京の胡同、樹木、屋根、壁の上が真っ白になった。

① 由于居住主人的习惯和爱好，一些南方建筑和外国建筑也出现在胡同中。看！这二层小楼的深宅大院，更显得新奇而神秘。

A two-story building in a compound. Along with the single-story houses unique to Beijing, structures built in southern and foreign styles can also be found on the hutongs.

住宅の主の習慣と愛好から、胡同の中に中国南部の建築と外国の建築も見られる。ごらんなさい。この奥まった二階建ての大邸宅は、いっそう新奇、神秘的に見える。

② 宣武区西南角的一座过街楼，它沟通了胡同两侧的宅院，使之成为一个整体。

An overhead building projection spanning a hutong in the southwestern Xuanwu District of Beijing.

宣武区の南西の隅にある通りをまたいている建築は、胡同両側の住宅と庭を通じさせ、一つの総体にしている。

雪后胡同更寂静

A tranquil and peaceful hutong in the snow

雪後の胡同はいっそう静かである。

雨中的胡同

A small hutong bending slightly at a tree.

雨天の胡同

蒋家大院，顾名思义，这里曾居住过一位姓蒋的知名人士。昔日深深的庭院，而今已分割成几个院落，但那高高的屋脊，阶前的花草仍能透出当年的几分风貌。北京的胡同名称中，有许多就是以当时住过的知名人士或家族来命名的。如班大人胡同、邓大人胡同、大方家胡同等。

Jiangjiadayuan (Jiang Family Compound) was probably the residence of a well-known person named Jiang. Although the compound has been partitioned into several smaller courtyard houses, the trees and flowers in the courtyard and the well-decorated roof ridges still give visitors an idea of its past splendor. In Beijing, many hutongs were named after prominent figures such as Bandaren (Lord Ban) Hutong, Dengdaren (Lord Deng) Hutong, and Dafangjia (Greater Fang Family) Hutong.

蒋家大院、名称から見ると、そこにかつて蒋という名字の有名人が住んだことがあると思われるが、この奥まった大邸宅もいまではいくつかの庭に分けられているが、高い屋根と建物の前に植えてある草花は往年の風貌をいくぶんか現している。北京の胡同の名称の中に、往時住んだ有名人やその家族の名前で命名されたものがたくさんある。例えば、班大人胡同、鄧大人胡同、大方家胡同などがそのいくつかの例である。

林木掩映下的简陋院门

A simple and crude front gate standing by old trees.

古い木は粗末な門とコントラストをなしている。

老胡同里的洋建筑

A group of Western-style structures in an old hutong.

古い胡同の中にある洋風な建物。

寓意“吉祥如意”的如意门，大多是清代和民国期间的建筑，当时的住户多为商人、艺人和退隐官宦等。

The richly decorated front gates of large courtyard houses are called ruyimen (good luck gate). Most courtyard houses with such gates were built during the Qing period or the Republican era. Their occupants were rich businessmen, famous artists, or retired officials.

「吉祥如意」の意味を含んでいる如意門は、たいてい清代と民国時期に建ったものであり、当時の住人は商人、芸人、引退した役人らであった。

高大的围墙，脱落的墙皮，展示着岁月冲洗的痕迹，但伸向墙外的长青藤，依然呈现着勃勃生机。

The plaster on the wall surrounding this courtyard house has worn off with time and weather but the ivy on it is still growing.

外側の層がはがれ落ちた高い壁は、歳月に洗い流された痕跡を示し、壁の外に伸びる藤のつるは依然として生気に満ちているように見える。

① 如意门前的古树，映衬出宅院历史的沧桑。摄于东城区盛方胡同。

The old trees are witnesses to the history of this courtyard house with a good-luck gate located at Shengfang Hutong in Dongcheng District,Beijing.

如意門の前にある古木は、歴史の移り変わりを現している。東城区盛方胡同で撮影。

② 高大门楼的檐角，门楣上精美的砖雕，显示着四合院主人的身份和雅兴。摄于后细瓦厂胡同。

The exquisite brick carvings on the gate tower of this courtyard house, located at Houxiwachang Hutong show the social status and artistic taste of their owner.

高くて大きい門楼のひさしの先端や門の上の横木の煉瓦彫刻は、四合院の主の身分と修養を顕示している。後細瓦廠胡同で撮影。

②

①

②

①② 昔日富户院落的大门，而今依然保留着八字粉墙。

The front gate of a courtyard house belonging to a rich family. It is flanked by white-washed walls shaped like the character "八".

昔は金持ちが住んだ邸宅の正門の両側に、いまでも八の字型の白い壁が保留されている。

宽亮的门楼，精美的砖雕，既反映了北京民居的风采，又展示了艺人的智慧。

An arch over a gateway embellished with elegant brick carvings.

広くて明るい門楼、精美な煉瓦彫刻は、北京の民家の風采と職人の知恵を現している。

风雪归人　Returning home in the snow.　吹雪の中に帰る人。

后海杨柳绿荫水曲弯弯，银锭桥畔烤肉香飘冉冉。

A city scene of Beijing showing homes surrounded by trees and a small stream spanned by a lovely bridge.

柳の木が陰をつくり、小さな流れの上に橋がかけてあり、そのたもとから焼肉の香りが漂ってくる。

古老的牌坊装点于幽深的胡同之中，这是北京独特的街市景观。过去，北京的东四牌楼、西单牌楼、前门五牌楼、北海桥头的金鳌玉蝀牌楼都十分有名。巍峨的牌楼，增强了街巷空间的艺术效果，体现了北京人的审美意蕴，也增加了北京古色古香的神韵。

Decorated archways are a scene unique to Beijing. They can be found on hutongs and streets. The best-known of them were the archways at Dongsi, Xidan, Qianmen, and the Beihai Bridge. They embody Chinese esthetics in architecture and add to the beauty of the ancient city of Beijing.

古い牌坊は静かな奥まった胡同の中で一つの飾りとなっている。これは北京でしか見られない街の風景である。以前、北京の東四牌楼、西単牌楼、前門五牌楼、北海の橋のたもとにある金鰲玉棟牌楼などはとても有名であった。高く立っている牌楼は通りと路地の空間の芸術的効果を大きくし、人の審美意識を体現し、北京の古めかしい雰囲気をいっそう濃くしている。

“宅子老不老，要看槐树大和小”。从门前这棵槐树和大门的门楼，可以判断出，当年这处宅院应是清代殷实富户所建。

"You can easily tell the age of a courtyard house in Beijing by the size of the trees in front of it," goes an old saying. Judging from the architectural style of the front gate and the size of the Chinese scholartree in front of it, this courtyard house must have been built by a rich family during the Qing period some one hundred years ago.

「住宅が古いかどうかは、槐の木が大きいかそれとも小さいかを見れば分かる」。門の前にあるこの槐の木と正門の門楼から、これが清代の金持ちの建てた四合院であると判断することができる。

一所宅院落成，门前往往要栽上两棵槐树，院子里也总要摆几盆花，像盆栽石榴树、夹竹桃，种在大鱼缸中的盆莲、慈姑什么的。

It was a common practice among Beijingers to plant two Chinese scholartrees in front of their new houses and Chinese flowering crabapples, bamboos, and pomegranate trees in their courtyards.

ある邸宅が落成すると、往々にして門の前に2株の槐の木を植え、庭の中に柘榴や夾竹桃の盆栽をならべ、魚を飼うかめの中に蓮や慈姑を植える。

老宅门墩

Courtyard houses are usually flanked by decorative stone sculptures.

旧い邸宅の表門の土台石。

便民
食品店
公用电话
各种冰棍
各种饮料
食品果品
冰镇啤酒
副食调料
上海平洋服装
SHANGHAI PIN PING GARMEN

昔日的繁华闹市、幽幽胡同里，也不乏二层小楼，别有一番情调。

Most of the two-story buildings on the hutongs in Beijing were built in the Republican era. Some of them are residential houses and others are lodging houses in downtown areas.

昔の賑やかな繁華街や静かな胡同の中に、二階建ての建物が少なからずあり、他のところと違うムードが漂っている。

修車

叩开四合院门

北京的胡同、四合院是老北京象征。

走进排列在胡同里的四合院，让人感到恬静而安详，这是老北京人理想的“安乐窝”。四合院有大、有小，但是都有一个被高墙封闭起来的疏朗的院落。正是这温馨、庄重的四合院，培养了一代又一代重礼仪、讲家教、有着浓厚传统文化积淀的北京人。

北京胡同中的大大小小的四合院（大的有王府、大宅门，小的有三合院、大杂院等）它们相辅相成，构成了多姿多彩的胡同景观。青砖灰瓦、玉阶丹楹，曲廊通幽，霞映屋宇。那高大的院墙挡住了街道的喧嚣，庭院内栽种的花木，更为小小的院落带来了勃勃生机。随着旧城的改造，一座新北京，一座国际化的大都市正日趋形成。而过去留下的四合院已经不多了。

走进胡同，古老的围墙在岁月的冲洗下已斑驳不平；院子的大门也已破烂不堪。然而，当人们高高兴兴迁往新居时，对这熟悉得不能再熟悉的老院落、老胡同，对这生活了几十年、几百年，经历了过多的酸甜苦辣，经历了过多风风雨雨的地方，总会产生几分眷恋之情，甚至会洒下怀旧之泪。

旅居海外的北京人，当月明星稀之夜，当独立寒秋之时，想起故园斑驳的砖墙，深邃的门洞，宁静的胡同，总会透出几分感慨、几分依恋。

漂泊四海的游子，回来吧！看看当年的旧居，看看今日的新北京；没有到过北京的五洲客人，欢迎您也来看看，可以在那胡同、四合院里，去搜寻源远流长的民俗佳话，去体验东方文化的情趣，其乐无穷。

Courtyard Houses

Beijing's courtyard houses, along with their hutongs, are symbols of old Beijing.

Beijing's courtyard houses are usually located on winding hutongs and have trees and flowers in their courtyards. Quiet and peaceful, they make ideal, cozy homes for Beijingers.

Courtyard houses in Beijing vary in size, but all have walls enclosing them. It is such mysterious, dignified yet comfortable courtyard houses that have helped bring up generation after generation of Beijingers who attach great importance to family education, etiquette, and traditional culture.

Beijing has a large number of courtyard houses on its hutongs, ranging from large, four-walled siheyuan which are former mansions of princes or the rich to three-walled sanheyuan which are now lived in by one or several families. Beijing's courtyard houses are built with gray bricks and roofed with gray tiles. The steps are made of marble and the pillars are painted vermilion. Most courtyard houses feature beautiful winding verandas and are designed to receive abundant morning light. As the high walls keep out the bustle of the city, the courtyard is quiet. Beijingers like to grow trees and flowers in their courtyards, making their homes lovely and pleasant.

With the reconstruction of the old city, Beijing is taking shape as an international metropolis, and its traditional courtyard houses are quickly decreasing in number. As housing is still a problem in Beijing, the siheyuan is now often shared by several families, and large parts of the courtyards have been taken over by families to build kitchens or additional rooms. Because of long years of weathering, the plaster on most walls surrounding Beijing's courtyard houses has peeled off.

Though a large number of Beijing residents have now moved to high-rises in new residential areas, their thoughts often go back to their old homes on the hutongs where their families lived for scores or hundreds of years.

A tour of Beijing's hutongs will enable Beijingers who have long been absent from their native town to relive the old days in their courtyard houses and to have a look at the new Beijing as well. It will also help tourists from foreign countries to gain an insight into Beijing folk life and Chinese culture.

四合院の門を開ける

北京の胡同と四合院は古い北京のシンボルである。

胡同の中に並んでいる四合院に入ると、静けさを感じ、安らぎを覚える。これは古い北京人にとって理想的な「安楽なねぐら」である。四合院は大きいものも小さいものもあるが、いずれも周りが高い塀に囲まれて、すっきりした庭がある。ほかならぬこの温かく、荘重な四合院で、礼儀と家庭のしつけを重んじ、濃い伝統的文化の内包をもつ北京人が次々と育てられたのである。

北京の胡同に大小さまざまな四合院があり、大きいものは王府(王族の邸宅)、大宅門(大きな屋敷)があり、小さいものは三合院、大雑院(一つの庭を囲んで立て込んだ建物に何世帯もの家族が住んでいるところ)などがあり、これらの四合院は互いに影響し合って発展し、多彩な胡同の景観をつくり出している。黒い煉瓦と灰色の瓦、白い階段と赤く大きな柱、曲がった廊下は静かで、建物は朝焼けと夕焼けで赤く染まる。庭を囲む高い塀は通りのやかましさを遮り、庭に植えた木や花は、小さな庭に生気をもたらしている。旧城の改造につれて、新しい北京、國際化した大都会が形成されつつあり、昔から残された四合院は少なくなった。

胡同に入ると、古い塀は歳月が経つにつれて、外側がはげ落ちて平らでなくなり、正門も原形をとどめないほど壊れている。しかし、人々は喜びにあふれて新居に引っ越す時、この隅から隅までよく知っている古い庭、古い胡同に対し、また数十年ないし数百年も暮らし、いくたの艱難辛苦をなめたところに対し、どうしても離れがたい気持ちになり、懐旧の涙を流す時さえある。

海外在住の北京人は、肌寒い秋の夜、月が昇り、星がきらめく夜、独り立っている時、以前住んだ家のまだらになった煉瓦の壁、奥まった表門、静かな胡同を思い出すと、感慨を覚え、名残を惜しむのはよくあることだ。

各地に漂泊している遊子たちは、帰ってきて、往年の旧居や今日の新しい北京を見てみるよう勧める。北京に来たことのない世界各地の賓客も、北京に来て参観するのを歓迎する。胡同や四合院で、昔から伝わってきた民俗の美談に耳を傾け、東方文化の情趣を味わうのもいいことで、限りなく楽しさを覚えるだろう。

虎头门钹

Door knockers shaped like tigers' heads.

虎の頭の形をした門の鉄輪。

夏日，坐在葡萄架下，也是惬意的享受。

It is a kind of enjoyment that sit under the grape vine in sweltering summer.

夏の日にブドウ棚の下に座るのも一種のすばらしい享受である。

瞧，端庄的如意门与简陋的陡墙厅，相互辉映，有多和谐。

A decorated front gate stands in sharp contrast to the small, shabby buildings on its sides.

荘重な如意門と粗末な陡墻庁は互いに照り映え、調和がとれている。

别看墙皮脱落，那加长的影壁， 仍显出官宦之家的气派。

Though it is broken,the unusual length of the screen wall suggests that the owner of the house was a high-ranking official.

表面が剥け落ちているが、長くなった目隠しの塀は、役人の家の気概を現している。

装饰独特的如意大门

An elaborately decorated front gate.

装飾が独特な如意大門。

残破的门钹，诉说着老宅的故事。

Broken cymbals with ring-shaped knockers on the front gate of an old courtyard house.

壊れた門の鉄輪は、古い住宅の故事を語っている。

庭院深深深几许

A residential compound with several courtyards.

庭は奥深いというが、どれくらい深いのか。

四合院小景

A small courtyard house.

四合院の風景。

格局独特的四合院建筑

A view of a courtyard house.

配置が独特な四合院の建築。

门前小巧的门墩儿，院内精致的影壁与高大的如意门楼，透出了昔日主人的家景。

The imposing front gate of a courtyard house belonging to a rich family. It is flanked by stone sculptures, and behind it stands a screen wall built with exquisite workmanship.

門前にある小ぢんまりとした精巧な土台石、庭の中の精巧な目隠しの塀と高くて大きな如意門楼は、昔の富裕な家の模様を現している。

这是过去官府或大宅门的宅院

A courtyard house belonging to an official or a man of influence.

昔の役所または大邸宅の庭

四合院转角处　　A turn in a courtyard house.　　四合院の曲がり角。

①② 中西合璧的四合院建筑

Houses in a courtyard built in a combination of Chinese and Western styles.

中（国）西（洋）折中の四合院の建築。

②

凉晒的衣服、堆放的大白菜、小院中充满生活味。

Sunned clothing and the pile of Chinese cabbages add to the courtyard's atmosphere of life.

洗った服が干され、白菜が積み上げられて、四合院の中庭は生活の息吹きにあふれている

雪后钟楼下的小胡同，显得更加静谧安详。

This hutong below the Drum Tower appears even more peaceful in the snow.

雪の降ったあと、鐘楼の下の小さな胡同はいっそう静かで落ち着いているように見える。

俯视成片的四合院，只见错落有致的屋脊好似灰色的波浪，起伏跌宕。

Roofs designed like surging waves.

北京の四合院を見下ろすと、入り混じって趣をなす屋根が灰色の波のように起伏し、とても特色がある。

带花园的大四合院一角

A view of a large res.dential house with gardens.

花園付きの大きな四合院の一角。

感受市井风情

The People and Folk Culture of Beijing

历史悠久的文化古都北京，既有大气磅礴的宫廷建筑，也有掩映于杨柳古槐之下的胡同，以及那出没于胡同、四合院中的形形色色的富有浓郁京味儿的北京人。

“东富西贵，南贱北贫”，这是一百多年前的清代，对北京“四九城”居民的概括。东富，是说一些巨商富绅都在东城居住；西贵，是指西城住的多为清朝的“显贵”；南城住有许多被视为下贱人的民间艺人和个体劳动者；北贫，是说北城交通闭塞，住的又多为满族八旗守城军士后裔，家道中落，日渐贫寒。“东富西贵”，到了1911年辛亥革命后又有所变化。由于军阀混战，一些夺得实权的达官新贵，大部分选择日渐繁华的东城居住。如，朝阳门内北小街的吉兆胡同有国务总理段其瑞的花园，东四六条流水巷有北洋军阀元老徐世昌的宅寓，铁狮子胡同有外交总长顾维均的私邸（孙中山先生来京也曾居住于此）。而一些富商巨贾则移居到商业繁华的西单、西四一带，他们修整庭院，装饰门楼，使西城一些街巷出现了“富”相，形成了“西富东贵”的新貌。南北城居住的则还是普通百姓。今日的北京市，除海淀区高科技园区和文教人员比较集中外，其他各区多为五方杂居，群贤相聚，呈现出一派团结和睦景象。

今日生活在北京的，是热情、善良、大方、豪爽的新北京人。清晨，数百万人骑着自行车、乘着公交车，开着小轿车，各自奔赴不同的工作岗位。傍晚，又返回胡同中自己的家园，为生活奏起锅碗瓢勺交响曲。月夜，胡同的路灯下，也会聚起一拨拨下棋的老人和观棋的君子，宽敞的空地上还有扭秧歌、练武术、跳集体舞的老大妈、小伙子。有时，小院中还会飘出京味浓郁的胡琴声和耳熟的西皮、二簧唱腔……

北京胡同的市井风情，串联起来，就像一幅绚丽多彩的民俗画卷。

Beijing is an ancient city rich in culture and history. It is famous for its magnificent palatial architecture and its unique hutongs and courtyard houses sheltered by the luxuriant foliage of willows and Chinese scholartrees.

A hundred years ago, during the Qing Dynasty, Beijingers used to say, "The rich live in the east, the officials live in the west, the poor live in the north, and the lowly live in the south. " During the Qing period, most wealthy merchants and businessmen lived in eastern Beijing and high-ranking officials had their homes in the western part of the city. Laborers and other people of the lowest social strata such as artisans and folk artists generally inhabited southern Beijing. With poor transport facilities, northern Beijing was where the poor descendants of the Manchu soldiers of Beijing lived in crowded conditions.

The situation changed after the 1911 Revolution. Those who came to power through wars between warlords chose to make their homes in the thriving eastern district of the city. For example, Premier Duan Qirui had a residence with gardens on Jizhao Hutong which intersects North Small Street inside the Chaoyangmen Gate; Xu Shichang, a senior politician of the Beiyang clique, lived in a courtyard house on Liushuixiang (Flowing-Water Alley) near Dongsiliutiao (Dongsi Archway No. 6 Alley); and foreign Minister Gu Weijun (Dr. Wellington Ku) had a private residence on Tieshizi Hutong (Iron Lion Alley), which also served as living quarters for Dr. Sun Yat-sen when he came to Beijing.

At the same time, rich merchants and businessmen began to move their homes to the downtown areas of Xidan and Xisi. They renovated their houses and erected imposing arches over the gateways. As eastern Beijing became the residential district for ranking officials, western Beijing gradually became the home of the rich. The housing conditions and the composition of the populations in the north and south districts of the city remained unchanged.

Today, apart from Haidian where people working in education and science and high technology are concentrated, the other districts of the city are inhabited by people of all walks of life.

Beijingers are friendly, straight forward, and honest. Many of them still live in hutongs. Some of them drive to work in the morning but most of them go by bicycle or bus. In the evening, they return to their courtyard houses to enjoy their home lives.

Community life in the evening is lively. Old men often have a game of chess under street lamps along the hutongs while people look on with great interest. On open grounds, you can find people dancing the yangge (a popular folk dance) or practicing martial arts. Sometimes the air is filled with the melodies of jinghu (a two-stringed bowed instrument used in Peking Opera) music and the songs of Peking Opera, which most Beijingers are familiar with.

市井の風情を味わい知る

長い歴史をもつ文化の古都北京には、この上なく精美な宮廷建築もあれば、柳や槐の木におおわれた胡同および四合院や胡同を行ったり来たりする北京の風儀に富む北京人もある。

「東富西貴」、「南賎北貧」。これは百余年前の清代の北京城の住民に対する概括である。「東富」とは金持ちの商人と紳士がみな東城(北京城内の東側)に住んでいることを言い、西貴とは西城には清朝の高位高官の名望家が大勢住んでいることを指し、南賎とは南城に卑しい人と見られた民間芸人と組織されていない勤労者が大勢住んでいることを言い、北貧とは北城の交通が不便で、住んでいる人がたいてい満州族八旗の北京城を守備する兵士の子孫であり、彼らの暮らし向きがわるくなる一方で、ますます貧しくなっていることを指す。1911年に辛亥革命が決行されてから、「東富西貴」に変化が現れた。軍閥の混戦で実権を握った新しい高官と貴人は大多数繁栄しつつある東城に住むようになった。例えば、朝陽門内北小街の吉兆胡同に国務総理段其瑞の花園があり、東四十六条の流水巷に北洋元老徐世昌の邸宅があり、鉄獅子胡同に外交総長顧維均の私邸がある。孫文も北京に来た時にそこに泊まった。一部の金持ちの商人は商業が繁華な西単、西四一帯に引っ越していき、庭の手入れをしたり、門楼を飾り立てたりして、西城の一部の通りや胡同に「富む」兆しを出現させ、「西富東貴」という新しい枠組みを形成した。南城と北城に住んでいるのは相変わらず一般庶民であった。今日では、海淀区にハイテクと文化・教育関係者が集中しているほか、その他の各区ではたいてい各方面の人が雑居し、多くの有能な人が集まり、団結し、仲よく付き合っている。

今日、北京で暮らしているのは正直、善良、熱情的、豪快な新しい北京人である。朝、数百万もの人が自転車やバスに乗ったり、マイカーを運転したりして、それぞれ自分の仕事場へ行き、夕方には胡同の中にある家に帰ってきて、家事をやり始める。月夜に、胡同の街灯の下で老人たちが集まって将棋をさし、ほかの人もたかって観戦し、広い空地では、人々が武術を習ったり、ヤンコーやスクエアダンスを踊ったりする。また庭から北京情緒たっぷりの胡弓の音と耳馴れた西皮、二簧の唱(うた)が伝わってきて、古い伝統と現代都市のリズムを一つに融け合わせる時もある。

北京の胡同に見られる市井の風情をひとつなぎにすれば、絢らん多彩な民俗絵巻となる。

幽静的胡同里，老人在门前悠闲地翻阅报纸，小儿在牙牙学语，构成了一幅“京城闲适图”。

A quiet and peaceful hutong.

静かな胡同では、老人が門の前でのんびりと新聞を広げ、赤子がアーアーといって言葉をまねている風景は、「北京の閑静でのどかな絵図」を構成している。

高墙房脊下的胡同风光

A narrow hutong.

高い壁と屋根の下にある胡同の様子。

夕阳下，高墙旁，这位老人安闲地躺在软椅上。他怀中的小半导体正在播送着传统京剧。他听得多么入神。

Sitting comfortably in a deck chair against the wall at nightfall, the old man listens to Perking Opera on his transistor radio.

夕方に、高い壁の下で、この老人は気楽に寝椅子の上に横わたり、胸のところにおいてある小さなトランジスタラジオが伝統的な京劇を放送し、老人は聞きほれている。

路灯辉映下的胡同里，两位老人棋兴正浓。路过观棋的，身临其境而不躁不惊。

A game of chess under a street lamp in a quiet hutong.

街灯に照らされる胡同で、二人の老人が対局に興じている。そばでそれを観戦している人は、いらだたず、驚かずに観ている。

街头理发师俗称剃头的，是北京传统的手艺人。而今，还能看到一个方凳，一块披巾，一把推子，就是一个简易理发摊儿的景观。

Traveling barbers can still be found in Beijing. They are equipped with only a square stool or a simple folding chair, a white cape, and clippers, and they offer their services under a tree or near the foot of a high wall where pedestrians are few.

街頭の床屋は俗に剃頭的と称され、北京の伝統的手芸人である。いまでも道具は腰掛け一つ、体を覆う布一枚、バリカン一つだけ、これが街頭床屋の景観である。

有时，高墙窄巷、人如潮流，这是节假日或上下班时最常见的。

It takes only a few people to make a crowd during rush hours and on holidays in hutongs, especially narrow ones.

高い壁の下の狭い道を、人々が潮のように行き来している。これは休日や出退勤の時に最もよく見かける胡同の風景である。

永清
食品店
电话
Tide
Tide
烟
天坛
今日起

胡同中的小卖部，俗称“小铺儿”，卖的是烟、酒、糖、茶、油、盐、酱、醋等生活用品。

Small shops in a hutong. Such shops sell articles of everyday use such as cigarettes, wines, sugar, tea, oil, salt, soy sauce, and vinegar.

胡同の中の小売部は「小鋪児」と称し、タバコ、酒、砂糖、茶、食用油、塩、醤油、酢などの生活用品を売っている。

节日的胡同

A hutong in holiday.

祭日の胡同の風景

这位修自行车的老人，也是个养鸟的行家里手。从挂在对面墙上的鸟笼中，传来阵阵婉转的鸟鸣声，使他忘记了生活的艰辛。

Hanging on a tree near the wall opposite the workshop of a bicycle repairman are two cages with birds. The singing of the birds relieves the repairman's fatigue.

この自転車修理の老人は鳥を飼う玄人である。向かい側の壁にかけてある鳥籠から伝わってくるのどかな鳥のさえずりを聞いて、暮らしの中の苦しみを忘れることができる。

搓煤球，也是老北京四合院里传统的家务劳动。但这早已是过去的事情了。

Making charcoal briquettes was part of the housework of most Beijing families in the mid-20th century. They depended on briquettes for cooking and heating.

豆炭づくりも昔四合院に住む人の家事労働であった。

雪中送炭

A young worker delivers honeycomb briquettes to a user in winter.

雪の中の練炭配達

砖墙下嬉戏的儿童

Children playing in a hutong.

煉瓦壁のそばで遊ぶ子供たち。

昔日北京胡同中,有许多庙宇建筑，多为高墙、崇阁、广殿。庙门内左右还建有钟、鼓二楼。这座破败的庙宇残迹，给古老的胡同带来了几分凄清之感。

A Buddhist temple in disrepair. Many Buddhist temples can be found in hutongs. Chinese Buddhist temples usually consist of a group of spacious halls and pavilions surrounded by a high wall. Standing on both sides behind the main gate are the drum and bell towers.

昔、北京の胡同の中に廟宇がたくさんあり、その多くは高い塀に囲まれ、高い閣楼や大きな殿堂があった。廟門の中の左右両側に鐘楼と鼓楼があった。この壊れた廟宇の遺跡は、古い胡同にいくぶんかのうら寂しい感じを与えている。

② 雪后即景

A hutong in the snow.

胡同の雪景色

① 磨剪子磨刀的，是走街串巷的传统手工劳动者。过去是扛着一条长板凳，上装磨刀石等工具，现在改为用自行车驮着磨刀工具，串游于小胡同中。

A knife-and-scissors sharpening man. In the past, they walked from house to house carrying a wooden bench fixed with a whetstone on their shoulders. Today they carry their tool-kits on bicycles.

はさみや包丁をとぐ人は胡同を歩き回る伝統的な手工勤労者である。以前は上に砥石などの道具を乗せた長い腰掛けをかついで歩いたが、いまは自転車に包丁を砥ぐ道具をのせて、小さな胡同をぐるぐる回っている。

胡同是北京最基层的行政区域，这里的居民一样享有自己的选举权。

Hutong is the smallest administrative division at the grass-roots level. People living there enjoy the right to vote their leadership.

胡同は北京の最も末端な行政区画で、そこに住む住民は同様に選挙権を享有している

北京“茶汤李”的小吃,很有名气。虽历经了百余年,传了两三代人,仍保持了传统风味。那把用于沏茶汤、高近一米的龙嘴大铜壶,被擦拭得闪闪发亮,格外引人。

Chatangli is a famous snack shop in Beijing. It sells mainly sweet paste and sweet dumplings made of glutinous rice flour in winter and bagao cakes and cold jelly in summer. The shop was opened by a person named Li more than 100 years ago. The huge, shining brass kettle is used for boiling water to make sweet paste.

北京の「茶湯李」の軽食は大変有名である。店は百年以上の歴史があり、経営者は2、3世代変わったが、相変わらず伝統的風味を保っている。高さ1メートル近くある竜嘴大銅壷はぴかぴかに磨かれて、ことのほか目に付く。

外国游人在普通百姓家中做客。那热气腾腾的饺子，可真够香的啊!

Foreign tourists entertained with Chinese dishes and meat dumplings in a Beijinger's home.

客として家に招いた外国観光客に、茹でたてのギョーザを出してもてなす。湯気の立つギョーザはおいしそうだ。

新春佳节，如意门上贴出大红对联，街上的欢闹声引出了两个小孩。那纯真的笑容，使古老四合院焕发出青春。

Hearing firecrackers exploding outside their house, two little children rush out to look, smiling happily. During the Spring Festival, people paste auspicious couplets written on red paper onto the gate posts or door panels to express their best wishes for the new year.

春節（旧正月）には、如意門に赤い紙に書いた大きな対聯がはってあり、路地の賑やかな声に引かれて二人の子供が出てきた。その無邪気な笑顔で、古い四合院は青春を取り戻したようである。

结婚，在老北京俗称“娶媳妇”，这是青年男女一生中的大事，也是胡同中老街坊们的喜事。新媳妇进门前，亲朋好友要把女方家中陪嫁的被褥、衣物以及电视、冰箱等送到男方家。这时的胡同，是热热闹闹，喜气洋洋。

Preparing for a wedding. Beijingers send the bride's trousseau including quilts, clothes, a television set, and a refrigerator to her husband's home before the wedding. When the bride and groom arrive, the groom's family and their friends will meet them at the gate of the house.

結婚は北京では俗に「娶媳婦」という。これは若い男女の一生のうちの大きな事であり、また同じ胡同に住む近所の人たちの喜ばしいことでもある。花嫁は門に入る前に、親友たちは嫁入り道具の夜具、衣類と冷蔵庫、テレビなどを新郎の家に送り届ける。その時の胡同は賑やかで、喜びにあふれている。

冰糖葫芦是老北京传统食品。吃在嘴里又凉又甜，还透着一点儿酸。

Sugarcoated haws on a stick are a traditional snack in Beijing. They have a sweet-and-sour taste.

氷糖葫蘆（山査の実を竹串にさし、煮てとかした砂糖をまぶし固めた菓子）は前前から北京の伝統的食品である。それを食べると口の中が冷たく、甘く、すっぱい味も少しまざっている。

热闹的春节庙会，吸引了成千上万的大人小孩。

A temple fair in Beijing during the Spring Festival.

賑やかな春節の縁日は、何千何万もの人を引き付けている。

晨光熹微的胡同中，老年、中年、青年人，以不同的形式锻炼身体。

Morning exercises.

夜が明けきらないうちから、老人、壮年、青年は異なる方法で体を鍛えている。

①

②

③

①②③ 胡同之夜

Night life in a hutong.

胡同の夜

如意门上的精美砖雕　Brick carvings over the front gate of a large courtyard house.　如意門の精美な煉瓦彫刻。

门墩，设于四合院大门门框两边，有装饰作用，门鼓上大多雕刻有石狮、花卉等。有的雕工十分精美。

The gate piers　Gate piers are usually set at both sides of the gate,and served as ornament with beautiful bas-relief carvings of lions and flowers.Made of stone,gate piers could firm the threshold up also.

門墩は四合院の表門の両側においてあり、装飾の作用を果たしている。門墩にはたいてい獅子や花卉などが彫つてあり、その中にとても精美なものもある。

图书在版编目(CIP)数据

北京胡同：画册／刘建斌等编. —北京：中国旅游出版社，2002.6

ISBN 7-5032-1996-3

Ⅰ.北… Ⅱ.刘… Ⅲ.①城市道路－北京市－画册②风俗习惯－北京市－画册 Ⅳ.K921-64

中国版本图书馆CIP数据核字(2002)第036549号

策　　划：杨　茵

中文撰稿：刘建斌

摄　　影：徐鸣雨、张肇基、徐　勇、杨　茵
陆　岩、陆　岗、王文波、郭　伟

责任编辑：吴建群、杨志敏

中文编辑：武冀平

封面设计：夏超一

装帧设计：众　志

英文翻译：崔思淦、王鹏

日文翻译：缪光祯

中国旅游出版社出版

北京华天旅游国际广告公司承制

开本：787×1092mm　1/12

印张：8　　印数：5000

2002年6月第一版第一次印刷

ISBN 7-5032-1996-3/K.577

0006000